D1565906

The Tail of the Raccoon
Part I

Secrets of Addiction

Other books by the Authors:

The Tail of the Raccoon, Part II: Touching the Invisible

The Tail of the Raccoon, Part III: Departures

The Tail of the Raccoon
Part I

Secrets of Addiction

A Scientific Short Story

Barbara Zito
and
Arthur Tomie, PhD

Cover Illustration by Steven James Petruccio

ZT Enterprises, LLC

Copyright © 1990, Barbara Zito and Arthur Tomie
First Printing 2014
ZT Enterprises, LLC (Publisher), 2014 Licensing Agreement
P.O. Box 2409
Princeton, NJ 08540
Publisher Web site: www.tailoftheraccoon.com
Publisher E-mail: ztenterprisesllc@gmail.com

Library of Congress Cataloging-in-Publication-Data
Barbara Zito, 1958-
Arthur Tomie, 1946-
        The Tail of the Raccoon, Part II: Touching the Invisible /
by Barbara Zito and Arthur Tomie. Includes Educational
Commentary, Scientific Commentary, Bibliographical
References, Glossary.
ISBN-13: 978-0-9913495-3-1
ISBN-10: 0-0991349539

For all those who serve.

Thank You

"Now when I hear Kiowa spoken - mostly by the older people who are passing away - it is to me very good. The meaning most often escapes me, but the sound is like a warm wind that arises from my childhood. It is the music of memory. I have come to know that much of the power and magic and beauty of words consist not in meaning but in sound."

N. Scott Momaday, "The Man Made of Words"

TABLE OF CONTENTS

Chapter One

••••••••••••••••••••••••••••

THE GREAT FOREST

The wigwam of Mapache could be found deep in the heart of the Great Forest, nestled within the confines of majestic towering cliffs. Thick was the forest with many varieties of trees and shrubs making it so dense that it was impassable to many travelers. However, despite the shadows that darkened much of the forest, within this beautiful spot beneath these sheer cliffs, sunlight found its way to the forest floor. Many flowers bloomed amongst the rocky crags at the foot of these cliffs, while birds built nests in the small crevices of the face. Mapache did not see the loveliness of the place in which he lived for he had been blinded by a blow to the back of the head in a fierce battle. Thus, the stunning beauty of his surroundings was in great contrast to the darkness in which he lived.

At the forest's edge was a great lake along whose rocky shores roamed the Raccoon. The Raccoon spent much of his time walking along the shores of the lake catching crayfish and washing them for food. He was muscular and strong and because of this, unlike many of his friends, he had no difficulty carrying a heavy burden. His legs were sturdy and feet so strong that he won many raccoon races. Not surprisingly, before long he had earned a reputation amongst his neighbors as being quite an extraordinary raccoon.

This particular Raccoon was widely considered to be one of the finest looking specimens of raccoons in the area. His fur was soft, fluffy, and of the finest color. He fancied himself to be one of the handsomest looking creatures in existence. He would often gaze into the surface of the lake where he could see his radiant image reflected in the water. He would prance up and down along the water's edge swishing his tail to and fro while singing:

"Such A Beautiful Creature Am I"

"I am so handsome
I am so strong
I am so handsome
My Tail is so long."

"These Rings on my Tail
They are so fine
These Rings on my Tail
My Tail is all mine."

Neighboring the Raccoon's haunts was a large encampment of tribal people, who, like the Raccoon, were privileged to live close to The Great Lake. They used the water for many purposes - drinking, bathing, fishing - and were quite pleased with what the lake provided. The people looked kindly toward Mapache and treated him well, although they could have chosen to leave him alone to despair over his troubles. Instead, his people who were known for their generous hearts, had worried that Mapache would be helpless in the case of another enemy attack and so they had decided to build him a wigwam in a quiet, remote region of the forest a good distance from their camp. There Mapache lived, sequestered from the rest of his people, though the people did not forget him. They provided him with supplies and utensils which were left close at hand so that he might be able to cook and care for himself. In a short time, however, they would have to make arrangements to leave him there safely while they moved their encampment in search of game.

As the people prepared to leave, Isquasis, their tribal medicine woman, reminded them that Mapache would need a helper to gather wood for his fire as they would be gone for an entire season. It occurred to them that their Raccoon neighbor might be able to help, so off they went in search of the Raccoon where they knew they would surely find him - along the water's edge. As they came closer to the Raccoon's home they heard his voice being carried over the water as he sang this song:

"So Many Crayfish"

"By the shore of the lake
At night I find
So many Crayfish
Out to dine."

"At the shore of the lake
Is where I'll be
So many Crayfish
Here for me."

The people soon came upon him busily engaged in cleaning the fish. He paused from his song and sat up on his haunches rubbing the fish between his front paws, stopping only to gnaw off bits of it. He washed and gnawed, washed and gnawed - eating insatiably while also keeping an eye on the approaching people. They greeted him in a very friendly manner and, after convincing him of their peaceful intentions, appealed to the very strong Raccoon to supply Mapache with firewood in their absence. The Raccoon pondered this idea for a moment, flicking his tail as he thought to himself, "I wonder how much trouble it will be to bring firewood to the dwelling of Mapache? No doubt the people will be exceedingly grateful to me for the favor!" Then suddenly his tail stopped moving. He had decided that he would try to satisfy the people's wishes because, although he loved crayfish, he was tired of eating only fish and hoped that the people might treat him to something especially delicious when they returned. And so the people were free to begin their journey, leaving Mapache in the Raccoon's care.

Mapache now lived quite comfortably. He had an abundant supply of wood provided by the hard working Raccoon and thanks to his kind-hearted friends, he had, close at hand, enough food and water to meet his needs. Thus satisfied, the world seemed a pleasant place to the blind man. He grew relaxed and content with this arrangement, while the Raccoon - assured that he was performing his job to the satisfaction of his charge - began to anticipate a well-deserved reward. As time went on Mapache developed a genuine fondness for the Raccoon and the Raccoon in turn continued to work diligently for him. Thus, it was, that through the kind thoughts and deeds of his friends, Mapache became more and more at ease in his cozy forest home.

Chapter Two

••••••••••••••••••••••••••••

A CELEBRATION OF THE HUNT

Days followed one after another, each a little shorter and a bit cooler than the one before, as autumn drew to a close. One fine day the people returned from their hunting expedition and arrived at The Great Lake laden with the spoils of a successful hunt. They carried with them game of various kinds ranging from buffalo, venison, and bear to small game such as rabbit and prairie chicken. A great deal of fatted meat had been transported back to the main camp to be roasted upon the open flames. The people celebrated and gave thanks for this food which meant very much to them indeed. In the evening you could see the fire light flickering against a background of shadows and twinkling stars. The camp was lit with bonfires as the people danced and rejoiced. All were happy and singing in a chorus of raised voices, giving praise to the Great Spirit for their exceptional good fortune.

The smells from the camp caught the attention of the handsome Raccoon as he lay in his den high above the forest floor in the hollow of a tree. He had worked hard for many days to supply Mapache with plenty of wood and now the smell of meat cooking drifted from the encampment and reached his ever vigilant nose. He twitched his nose quizzically in many directions appraising all of the various smells that reached him. He was clearly pleased with the result. Many delicious morsels were being divided amongst the people. The smell of fat sizzling on charcoal wafted past his hungry nostrils while the sounds of the people rejoicing filled his ears. These aromas and sounds instantly dispelled any doubts he had about the richness of the reward he would soon be given. He licked his lips in anticipation and fell asleep dreaming of the luscious foods that the people would soon deliver to Mapache and himself.

Chapter Three

••••••••••••••••••••••••••••••••

GREETING FRIENDS

Mapache was sitting outside his home relaxing in the warm sunshine when a group of the people came through the woods to greet him. They were glad to find him in good health and good spirits. Mapache told them how the Raccoon had done a fine job of supplying him with plenty of dry wood and how the fires he had been making were kindled up quickly - with very little smoke. He told the people that he would gladly repay the Raccoon for his efforts, if he had the means. The people readily agreed that this should be done and assured him that they would provide him with a large cache of food so that he might have plenty of provisions for himself and his Raccoon friend.

The people led horses to the wigwam of the blind man packed with the goods they had collected. Among the bundles were smoked and salted meats, fish, pemmican, corn, and various fruits, nuts and berries. The people worked together to provide Mapache with the necessities he would need to carry him through the coming months. The women sewed new leather leggings and sturdy moccasins for him. They checked to be sure that he had a plentiful supply of rainwater, sound cooking utensils and warm blankets. The people worked tirelessly and were steadfast in their desire to see that all was well.

The kind words and deeds of his people filled the heart of Mapache with joy. This feeling of lightness prompted him to eagerly await the arrival of the Raccoon so that he might share in the bountiful harvest with him. Mapache was very grateful to the Great Spirit for providing him with friends such as these and resolved to express his appreciation by behaving in a like manner toward the hard working Raccoon.

The people did not plan to venture out to check on Mapache for a long time after this and so they persevered in making sure that everything was in order. Mapache explained to them, with great certainty, that they should not be concerned that his supply of firewood would become depleted. He explained that the Raccoon was a very dependable worker, and, after all, he was planning to bolster the Raccoon's interest by treating him to some tasty morsels the next time he stopped by with a supply of wood. What could possibly go wrong with an arrangement that would be advantageous to both of them? Assured of the sound judgment of Mapache - based on the positive experiences he had, thus far - the people were convinced that he would continue to receive an ample supply of dry firewood from their neighbor the Raccoon.

As the people packed up their horses and prepared to travel back through the woods once again, Mapache was beside himself with gratitude. After exchanging goodbyes with Mapache the people departed from his home and disappeared into the deep shadows of The Great Forest leaving Mapache to stand outside his wigwam - his face lifted to the sun - offering up a prayer to the Great Spirit to look after his people on their long journey home.

Chapter Four

....

THE PAIRING OF
WOOD AND FOOD

In the warmth of the sun close to the water's edge, the Raccoon lay on his back sleeping, his head propped up against a log and his forepaws covering his eyes. Now and then he stirred restlessly until a cold wind coming up over the water awakened him. He stood up and stretched himself, yawning and rubbing his eyes. In a moment he was fully alert and feeling a chill in the cool, brisk, breeze. He remarked to himself, "This cold air reminds me that Mapache must be in need of some more firewood. No doubt the people have visited him by now and have left him with fresh supplies, some of which may be for me!" And so the Raccoon began to gather pine cones, kindling sticks and larger pieces of wood to carry over to the dwelling of Mapache.

It was not long before the Raccoon had gathered a sufficient amount of wood to make his trip. He lifted it upon his back and headed through the forest. He knew the way quite well and found it a simple matter to haul the wood over rocks and trees. He soon arrived at his destination and in his usual way piled up the wood outside the door of the wigwam underneath an overhanging awning. Suddenly his senses became alerted to the smell of something unusual. "Aha!" he exclaimed, "Mapache must have left some treats for me somewhere close by." He followed his nose and swiftly located the goodies on a shelf above the wood pile. There he uncovered a platter of sweet corn and buffalo meat prepared by Mapache along with some pemmican that had been prepared by the women. His mouth watered at the sight of the food and its wonderful aroma. Without a moments hesitation he began taking huge mouthfuls of food, devouring all he could find. The pemmican was especially delicious. It was made of lean dried meat, pounded fine by the women, and mixed with maple sugar and melted fat. The Raccoon had never tasted such a scrumptious combination of tasty morsels. He searched for Mapache and looked about for more goodies, but could find neither. Finally, he decided that he could do nothing more at the moment and so he headed back through the forest the way he had come.

Now that the Raccoon had tasted some of the Indian's food and had experienced it's unusual kind of richness, his thoughts often turned to the prospect of getting his paws on some more. This thought became foremost on his Raccoon mind and so he planned to make another trip to the home of Mapache very soon. The Raccoon wasted no time in collecting more branches and kindling sticks. Again he arrived at the usual place and unloaded the wood, and again he found a delicious meal waiting for him. This time he allowed himself more time to savor the morsels. The hungry Raccoon picked up the corn cob and twirled it about with his forepaws. He nibbled off some of the kernels of corn and then twirled it about some more. "I could get used to eating this yummy food," said the Raccoon cheerily, "Yum! Yum! Yum! It is mouth-watering delicious." The Raccoon continued to indulge in the goodies that had been left, greedily lapping up every last bit on the plate. When he was convinced that none of the meal remained, he headed back to his native haunts, thoughts of gathering more wood already entering his mind.

The Pairing of Wood and Food

For several days this pattern continued, the Raccoon bringing wood to the wood pile and the reward always waiting for him when he finished his work. Each time he arrived with a load of wood he discovered a tasty morsel that appealed to him very much. It was not long before the Raccoon began to anxiously anticipate his trips through the woods to the home of Mapache. He now spent much less time hunting crayfish so that he could spend more time gathering wood in order to gain these exceptional taste treats. He would hastily gather up pine cones and sticks of various sizes searching endlessly for more wood. Before long he was constantly handling sticks and wood to the point that he did very little else.

Chapter Five

....

A PRAYER IS SAID

One very cold winter day Mapache went out to the wood pile in order to bring in some wood to stoke up his fire. He reached into the pile and picked up a piece of wood that felt very strange. "This is not the same type of wood that I have been getting," he thought quizzically. He felt the stick with his hands. It was wet and the bark had been taken off. He knew that this stick would not burn very well and so he put the stick down and searched about for drier wood. He managed to find enough dry wood to build up his fire, but was puzzled as to why some of the wood was in such poor condition.

The next day Mapache went out to the wood pile and was dismayed to find that the little wood that remained was in terrible condition. Wet and shredded it appeared to have been mangled and stripped. Mapache began to worry. What was happening he did not understand, but the result was easy to foretell. This wood would burn very poorly - if at all - and would make a very smoky fire. "Why is this wood in such poor condition," he thought, "when things have been going so well up until now?" He did not know the answer, but knew that the Raccoon had been making many haphazard trips to the wood pile lately and had been eating every scrap of food that was given.

As days went by the condition of the wood grew progressively worse. Soaking wet, the bark stripped off and broken into small pieces, it was a sorry stack of firewood. Mapache thought to himself, "If the Raccoon continues to bring me wood such as this, there will be plenty of trouble for me. Perhaps the treats I have given him are not a satisfactory reward for the hard work he has been doing and this is his way of telling me. I will leave out more of my food and this will surely please him. I'm certain that after he is rewarded justly he will bring me some good dry wood as he did in the beginning." The following day with hopes raised and expectations high Mapache went out to check his wood pile. Unfortunately, he discovered that his plan had not helped the situation and had only made matters worse. He found very little wood remaining the next day and what was left was merely shreds of wet sticks. This was all that remained of what was once a well stocked wood pile.

The nights grew colder and snow began to fall heavily. The cold winds blew the snow into high drifts as the trees popped and snapped in the bitter cold. Mapache wrapped himself in blankets and lay under his heavy buffalo robe. The smoke of his dwindling fire was thick and black causing him to choke quietly. Mapache now found himself in dire straits as the air grew colder and his fire started to die out. "With no wood for the fire, surely I will freeze to death!" he cried out, his body shivering. "Oh, Great Spirit, is it your will that today should be my last day on earth? Is this the place that you have chosen, where I must face my final hour? Oh, Great Spirit, please hear my prayer, have mercy on me and save me from this cold and lonely death."

Chapter Six

....

STRANGE BEHAVIOR, INDEED

Far away from the wigwam of Mapache in the main camp of the people, Isquasis, the medicine woman tossed and turned in her sleep. Troubled by her dreams, she awakened with a start and felt a numbing chill go through her body. In her dreams she had seen a night sky - without any stars - and black smoke eerily rising and then vanishing into it. Very disturbed was Isquasis by this awful omen and so she wrapped herself up tightly in heavy furs and stepped outside to look up at the early morning sky. Gazing upward above the trees she spotted the slightest trace of black smoke a great distance away.

Calling to the others to arise and investigate this strange phenomenon, Isquasis soon had a large group of people before her. She told them of her dream and said that she thought this smoke was coming from the direction in which Mapache lived. None knew or had heard of any problems with Mapache, but some children spoke up and told her that they had seen his helper, the Raccoon, in the forest lurking about a stream. They told her excitedly that they had seen him running about as if he had lost his senses. His fur was messy and he sang off key. He acted in odd ways, racing about with all kinds of wood in tow, dragging it about and washing it in the stream.

The medicine woman contemplated this information for a moment and then decided that she had better go off and see the Raccoon for herself. She followed a trail along a stream that snaked its way through a dark and dreary part of the forest. When she came upon the Raccoon she saw that he appeared just as the children had portrayed. She found the Raccoon at the water's edge washing sticks and gnawing on them as if they were crayfish. Frantically he raced about collecting wood of all kinds, climbing up and down trees and gnawing off branches and twigs. She watched him as he gathered the wood together and hauled it into the stream to wash. "Strange behavior is this, indeed," thought Isquasis as she watched the Raccoon curiously running about. She noticed how dull his fur looked, how thin his legs were, and the darting movements of his eyes. Isquasis was convinced that the Raccoon had no control over his own actions. He had been transformed into another being that was completely absorbed in the gathering of every branch and twig in sight. How and why this had come about she continued to ponder, but one fact stood out above all others and did not escape her keen sight - the Raccoon's tail did not move and had lost all of its rings.

Watching his every movement and listening closely to him as he raced about, she could hear him muttering to himself, almost like singing, but in a monotonous way:

"Over and Over and Over Again"

"To the stream I go
With a branch in tow
Over and over and over again
To the stream I go."

"Up and down the tree
Wood is here for me
Over and over and over again
Up and down the tree."

The medicine woman was beginning to decipher the import of this unusual behavior. "I must gather a party of the people," she thought, "and we must go to the home of Mapache. I fear that he is in great danger." And so the medicine woman rushed back to the main camp and gathered a rescue party together. They prepared hurriedly because the uneasiness of Isquasis told them that there was no time to waste. Before the sun had risen to its zenith, they had taken up the trail that led to the place where Mapache lay freezing and silent.

Chapter Seven

....

JOY - TO BE FREE

The people struggled through the forest on snowshoes working desperately to reach the secluded home of Mapache. They led one horse after them dragging a travois loaded with their necessities. Many hours passed in the bitter cold before they began the final leg of their journey. As they drew closer to their destination they used up most of their energy fighting off the cold and bitter winds. Numb with cold themselves, they arrived to find Mapache barely breathing. It took them no time at all to realize that Mapache had used up all of his firewood and that the remnants of wet wood that remained were the source of the heavy smoke that Isquasis had seen in her dreams.

A few of the people set out to search for some dry sticks to kindle a fire while the others cared for Mapache. Soon they had a crackling fire burning inside the wigwam. Gradually they added sticks to the fire which continued to brighten, casting a golden glow across each attentive face. Isquasis drew Mapache closer to the fire and massaged his limbs. Slowly his blood warmed and his heart pumped with renewed vigor. When it seemed that he had passed through his most dire moments, Isquasis left him where he lay and walked outside. She returned with a pot filled with snow and placed it near the fire to melt. She then added whatever food she had at hand to the water in order to make a broth that would warm everyone as they kept a watchful eye on Mapache who lay near the fire, slowly coming to life.

When Mapache recovered enough to realize that he had been saved, he wept with a mixture of joy and sorrow.

"I am not worthy of your efforts," he cried, "I am a fool! You should not risk your lives to save one such as mine."

After Mapache had regained control of his senses he explained to them what had transpired and how he had given the Raccoon the best food he could spare in order to induce him to maintain a constant supply of firewood - but to no avail. "There were those among you who warned me that I would need more help through these cold winter months than a lone raccoon could provide," explained Mapache. "But I, thinking that I could make do without the aid of my friends, turned them away. Oh, how little I know now and how little I knew then! You see me here. You see the result of my foolish ideas. Such is the fate of this blind man.

To be an object of pity to the people he loves. You should have left me to die, my friends. You should have left me to die, alone with my foolish ideas."

Isquasis spoke to Mapache and tried to console him. "You can not be expected to see as we do, Mapache," said Isquasis gently. "I, myself, did see the Raccoon with my own eyes. What they revealed to me is that he is as near to death as you are. He has lost all the Rings on his Tail. There can be no doubt that the strong and true spirit he once had has left him. We should have known better than to leave you here by yourself with only the Raccoon to rely on."

"But, why?" questioned Mapache. "Why has he weakened so when I provided him with some of my finest morsels?"

"I am sorry," explained Isquasis. "It seems that his raccoon mind imagines the kindling wood to be delicious food. He acts very strangely and has turned his attention to the wood in a way very odd to see. He is endlessly trying to devour it. If you had eyes that could see, you would be amazed to watch how he gnaws and handles the wood as though it were crayfish."

"Is there no help for him?" asked Mapache sadly. "I feel that I am the reason he has been transformed in this unusual way. It was because he was asked to help me that he has come to this. How terrible! To have lost all the Rings on his Tail. Please say that you can help him Isquasis. He must not remain so attracted to the wood that his very life will cease. My Raccoon friend does not deserve to have his life end this way."

Isquasis spoke once more before leaving Mapache to sit and to wonder, "He is a Tracker of the Sign - that is what you must know. This seems very strange to all who have witnessed it, but it is true nonetheless. He has become a Sign Tracker, but there is still hope for him."

After several days had passed and Mapache was recovered sufficiently, the people wrapped him in furs and lifted him onto the travois, fastening him securely. They had decided that it would be best if they brought him back to the main camp with them so that he could have plenty of time to recover. Meanwhile, Isquasis sought out the Raccoon by the stream where she had last seen him. He looked weaker than ever, and appeared to be quite ill. His fur was dull and dirty. He wobbled about on his feet, unsure of himself like a child who is lost. His youthful exuberance and vitality were gone, replaced by a body that was nothing more than a hollow shell. His eyes had no life in them and could only stare dimly. Isquasis was filled with pity for the Sign Tracker and sought to remove him from this place. With soothing words she convinced him to lay down his wood and follow her.

Isquasis hid the Sign Tracker away from all disturbances for three days. She fed him small bits of crayfish and brushed his fur until it began to shine again. She wrapped each of his paws in a poultice because they were calloused and scraped from rubbing the wood for so long. He lay back blankly staring into the sky, oblivious to the actions of Isquasis. He constantly muttered to himself in confusion, but eventually Isquasis was able to make sense of some of his words which sounded something like this:

"Not Mine"

"Here by the lake
I was handsome and strong
Feeding on Crayfish
All the night long."

"Then came the food
So tasty, so fine
No Rings on my Tail
My Tail is not mine."

Isquasis looked upon the Sign Tracker with compassion and mercifully tended to him for several days. She went into the forest and collected various medicinal roots and herbs in order to make him a healing broth. Isquasis never wavered from her determination to help the Raccoon recover and before long the Sign Tracker had regained some of his strength. His taste for crayfish improved and the Rings on his Tail started to reappear, even darker than they were before. Thanks to the efforts of Isquasis he improved greatly and became more like his old self again, but something was different.

The Raccoon had become more experienced and wiser. He remembered the tasty treats all too well, but fortunately for him, he did not forget that the thoughtlessness brought about by his obsession for these tasty morsels had completely taken over his life. "Never again will I surrender the Rings on my Tail," he vowed. "Mapache, I still think fondly of, and I know that the treats he provided for me would taste as delicious today as they did then, but I have learned that I must never indulge in them again. Never will I travel upstream to the place where there is no sun to warm me. I know I would be swept away by impulses that I am powerless to overcome."

And so it was that Sign Tracker matured into an older and wiser raccoon. The people called him by this new name because of the odd way in which he had behaved. The children especially liked to sit at night around the camp fires and listen to Mapache tell the story of his adventures with Sign Tracker. Though he could not see, Mapache had learned a lesson about the Rings on the Raccoon's Tail, just as the children learned lessons about the world around them every day. Mapache never failed to end his story by giving thanks to the Great Spirit for sending his people to rescue both himself and Sign Tracker from the events of those terrible days.

Sign Tracker's song was never quite the same after this. It still sounded beautiful and melodious, but in a different way. It was not the song of his carefree youth. He would relax in the sunshine by the side of the lake occasionally noticing his reflection on the rippling surface of the water. He would quietly sing to himself like this:

"Joy - To Be Free"

"Happy was I
Light and carefree
Feeding on Crayfish
A joy
Just to Be."

"Now I am older
Wiser, that's me
Feeding on Crayfish
A joy
To Be Free."

~ THE END ~

EDUCATIONAL COMMENTARY

....

Sign-Tracking: The Symbol and the Reward

by

Arthur Tomie, Ph.D. & Barbara Zito

"The Tail of the Raccoon: Secrets of Addiction" is a scientific short story. The story was developed by Professor Arthur Tomie, an addiction research scientist at Rutgers University, in collaboration with Barbara Zito, an author and editor. They have pooled their talents to bring a behavior called Sign-Tracking to the attention of the general public.

One of the reasons why Sign-Tracking behavior fascinates people is because it defies logic. To the casual observer, Sign-Tracking behavior can seem peculiar. Sign-Tracking is described in "The Tail of the Raccoon: Secrets of Addiction" when a symbol (kindling wood) is seen just prior to receiving a reward (Mapache's food). After this happens over and over again, the wood becomes a symbol of reward and the Raccoon begins to behave toward the kindling wood as though it was the actual food reward. This behavior, to act toward a symbol as though it is an actual reward, is called Sign-Tracking. It is apparent when the symbol of reward controls behavior. As described in the story, Sign-Tracking did not help the Raccoon get the food, rather the Raccoon's Sign-Tracking behavior drew his attention away from the food reward. The Raccoon gnawed and chewed on the sticks, then dragged them into the lake, and splashed them about in the water. These peculiar actions are a waste of time and energy, and serve only to delay the eating of the real food rewards, to say nothing of their effects on the quality of Mapache's fire.

It is especially difficult to understand the actions of the Raccoon because we know two important facts. First, that he loves Mapache's delicious foods, and second, that his Sign-Tracking behavior becomes hurtful and results in the deterioration of the Raccoon's health. Nevertheless, the intention of the Raccoon, to devour those tasty treats, is thwarted by his impulse to eat the reward symbol. The lesson of the story is that there is a disconnect between the intention of the Raccoon, to eat the delicious food, and the action of the Raccoon, to perform Sign-Tracking, and this is due to the enormous power of the reward symbol.

To learn more about how Sign-Tracking plays a role in the drug addiction process, read "The Tail of the Raccoon, Part II: Touching the Invisible" and "The Tail of the Raccoon, Part III: Departures". Additional information about Sign-Tracking and drug addiction is also available at our website:

www.tailoftheraccoon.com.

SCIENTIFIC COMMENTARY

....

Sign-Tracking:
Unmasking the Secrets of Addiction
by
Arthur Tomie, Ph.D. & Barbara Zito

This story introduces the reader to the phenomenon of "Sign-Tracking", as revealed by the behavior of "Sign Tracker" the Raccoon character and protagonist of the story. Sign-Tracking is observed when animals repeatedly experience pairings of a small object with a food reward. As revealed by the story, this experience leads to the development of feeding behavior directed

at the small object predictive of the food.
Sign-Tracking has been widely reported by behavioral
scientists studying the effects of this type of Pavlovian
conditioning procedure; thus, the strange behavior of
"Sign Tracker" is based, in part, on research findings
published in scientific journals.

The Raccoon in the story exhibits several features
of the Sign-Tracking phenomenon:

1.   The Raccoon's Sign-Tracking behavior develops
        after he has experienced repeated pairings of the
        kindling wood (reward symbol) with the food
        (reward substance).

2.   The Raccoon is compulsively drawn to the
        reward symbol (kindling wood) as though unable
        to impede the performance.

3.   The Raccoon behaves toward the kindling wood symbol <u>as though it were actually food</u>, i.e., salivating and gnawing on the kindling wood symbol.

4.   The Raccoon actually <u>loses many possible food rewards</u> because he becomes so involved in symbol-directed behavior.

The behavior of the Raccoon in the story is patterned after descriptions provided by Keller and Marian Breland (1961, 1966), who were professional animal trainers, with experience training thirty-eight species of animals, totaling over 6,000 individual animals. They reported that while they were able to train animals to perform various tasks, they "... ran afoul of a persistent pattern of discomforting failures. These failures, ... fall into a very interesting pattern."

This pattern is revealed by the Breland's descriptions of the behavior of their raccoons. The Brelands, like Mapache, attempted to induce a raccoon to deliver a small piece of wood in exchange for food reward. The raccoons trained by the Brelands were easily taught to pick up wooden coins and deposit them through a slot into a small metal box for food reward; however, with continued training the raccoons gradually ceased performing the task. Curiously, they now seemed unable to let go of the coins, spending several minutes handling them with their forepaws and rubbing them together "in a most miserly fashion". They often dipped the coins into the slot but then pulled them out again. After repeated pairings of the wooden coins with food, the coins were rarely deposited. Instead, they were picked up by the raccoons and chewed, licked, scratched, clawed, rubbed, and "washed". Remarkably, the actions the raccoons directed at the wooden coins made it appear as though they were trying to remove the exoskeleton of a crayfish. The Breland's encountered this same sort of problem in a variety of other species, including chickens, pigs, dolphins, and whales. In each case, the training began well. Virtually any animal can be trained to hand over a symbol in order to receive a food reward; however, after extensive training, virtually every animal that has been studied begins to "misbehave". The behavior initially learned - relinquishing the symbol in order to gain a food reward - seldom occurs. In its place are persistent patterns of feeding behaviors typical of the species and directed at the symbol of reward. Ironically, the behavior seems to serve no other purpose than to delay the delivery of the food reward itself.

Just as Pavlov's dogs developed the tendency to salivate upon merely hearing the tone that preceded food, the Raccoon of the story washes and gnaws on the symbol of reward as though it were actually food. The Brelands labeled this pattern of activity "misbehavior" because the actions required greater physical output and served only to delay, sometimes endlessly, the time for the delivery of the actual food reward. This behavior should not be interpreted as the distraction of an animal that has lost interest in eating, because increasing the animal's hunger merely intensifies the effect.

The performance of Sign-Tracking behavior does not appear to be under the voluntary control of the subject. If it were, the subject would be expected to simply not do it, particularly when the performance serves no purpose other than to deprive the subject of the actual reward itself. Nevertheless, subject after subject, in species after species, behave in this odd way, losing the majority of their food rewards by failing to restrain the tendency to display

Sign-Tracking behavior when they are in the presence of the reward symbol. The behavior of the Raccoon character in "The Tail of the Raccoon: Secrets of Addiction" is modeled after descriptions of Sign-Tracking behavior found in scientific journals. This phenomenon has been described by research scientists who have studied the effects of pairing small symbols with rewarding substances. Research such as this provides compelling testimony to the power of reward symbols and their ability to control and to direct behavior.

Sign-Tracking is important because it provides us with a way of understanding how behavior can become irrational and defy free will. Consider the intention of the Raccoon. The Raccoon is very much interested in eating Mapache's delicious treats, but eventually, after many pairings of wood and food, his intention to devour those tasty morsels is seldom observed. Instead, his actions are those of Sign-Tracking. The disconnect between the Raccoon's intentions and the Raccoon's actions are not unlike those of the drug abuser, who intends to restrain drug-taking, but, instead, finds himself or herself unable to control the impulse to have yet another.

Scientific studies suggest that Sign-Tracking contributes greatly to the uncontrolled drug-taking of the addict. Sign-Tracking induces loss of control of action directed at the object that signals reward. This pretty much summarizes the essence of the problem of the drug addict. The drug addict is unable to control their drug-taking. They take the drug even when they are trying not to, and like Sign-Tracking, their drug-taking consists of action directed at the object that signals the reward. For example, drug addicts exhibit the symptoms of Sign-Tracking after they experience the object (cocktail glass) as a signal for reward (alcohol). In the presence of the cocktail glass they are drawn toward the glass, and cannot resist reaching out and drinking from the glass. This suggests that the secret of addiction, the overlooked basis for the uncontrolled drug-taking of the addict, is Sign-Tracking of drug-taking.

To learn more about Sign-Tracking and addiction, read "The Tail of the Raccoon, Part II: Touching the Invisible" and "The Tail of the Raccoon, Part III: Departures". Additional information about Sign-Tracking and drug addiction is available at our website: www.tailoftheraccoon.com.

Suggested Readings:

Breland, K., & Breland, M. (1961). The misbehavior of organisms. The American Psychologist, 16, 681-683.

Breland, K., & Breland, M. (1966). Animal behavior. New York: Macmillan.

Brown, P. L., & Jenkins, H. M. (1968). Auto-shaping of the pigeon's key-peck. Journal of the Experimental Analysis of Behavior, 11, 1-8.

Tomie, A., Brooks, W., & Zito, B. (1989). Sign-Tracking: The search for reward. In S. B. Klein & R. R. Mowrer (Eds.), Contemporary learning theories: Pavlovian conditioning and the status of traditional learning theory, (pp. 191-223). Hillsdale, N.J.: Lawrence Erlbaum Associates, Publishers.

Young, Egerton R. (Ed.) (1903). *Algonquin Indian Tales*. New York: Fleming H. Revell Company.

GLOSSARY

Cache: A collection of items of the same type stored in a hidden or inaccessible place.

Console: Comfort (someone) at a time of grief or disappointment.

Crayfish: Also called crawfish or crawdads. A freshwater shrimp. Crayfish are a favorite food of raccoons.

Decipher: Succeed in understanding, interpreting, or identifying (something).

Deplete: to decrease seriously or exhaust the abundance or supply of.

Diligent: having or showing care and conscientiousness in one's work or duties.

Dispel: Make a doubt, feeling, or belief disappear.

Encampment: A place with temporary accommodations consisting of huts or tents, typically for troops or nomads.

Foretell: Predict the future or a future event.

Import: to be of consequence or importance to; matter, concern.

Insatiable: an appetite or desire impossible to satisfy.

Isquasis: Algonquian Indian name. In the Ojibwe language, ikwezens - pronounced ih-quay-zayns. Isquasis is the name of a Native American female character in the book, "Children of the Forest" by Egerton R. Young. Medicine women of Native American tribes were noted for their powers of healing.

Mapache: Spanish for raccoon. Adopted from the Aztecs, meaning "[the] one who takes everything in its hands".

Monotonous: (of a sound or utterance) lacking in variation in tone or pitch.

Omen: An event regarded as a portent of good or evil.

Pemmican: A concentrated mixture consisting of lean meat dried, pounded fine, and mixed with melted fat. It is prepared in different ways for use as a nutritious and energy-rich food. Orignally prepared by the native peoples of North America.

Poultice: A soft, moist mass of material, typically of plant material or flour, applied to the body to relieve soreness and inflammation and kept in place with a cloth.

Ponder: Think about (something) carefully, especially before making a decision or reaching a conclusion.

Prairie Chicken: Also called Pinnated Grouse. A large bird of the grouse family, native to the woodlands and prairies of North America.

Provision: The action of providing or supplying something for use.

Quizzical: (of a person's expression or behavior) indicating mild or amused puzzlement.

Remnant: A small remaining quantity of something.

Secluded: (of a place) not seen or visited by many people; sheltered and private.

Sequestered: (of a place) isolated and hidden away.

Steadfast - Resolutely or dutifully firm and unwavering.

Transpire: Occur; happen.

Travois: A triangular frame structure consisting of a platform or netting mounted on two long poles used by North American Indians to drag loads over land.

Venison: The meat of a wild game animal, especially a deer.

Vigilant: Keeping careful watch for possible danger or difficulties.

Wigwam: A domed, round shelter. Single-room dwelling place of the Native American Indians, typically an arched framework of poles overlaid with bark, rush mats, or hides.

Zenith: The highest point reached by a celestial or other object.

Made in the USA
Middletown, DE
28 June 2023

34050343R00047